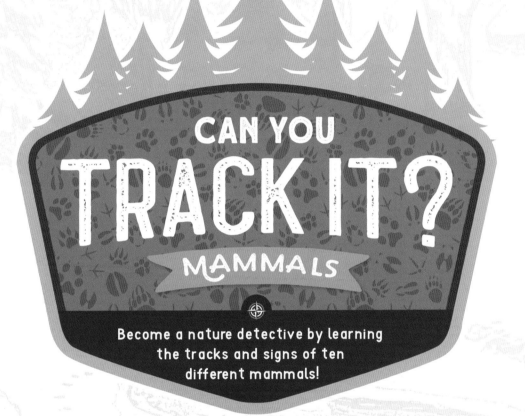

CAN YOU TRACK IT?

MAMMALS

Become a nature detective by learning the tracks and signs of ten different mammals!

Written by

Maggie Felsch and Shannen Yauger

Illustrated by

Tanya Glebova and Abram Felsch

Design and layout by

Phillip Colhouer

Have you ever noticed animal tracks in the mud or the snow? Do you know what animal left those tracks? Did you pause to consider where that animal was going, what it was doing, or where it lived? A tree with claw scratches, a tuft of fur, a paw print, or a dropped feather may be all you have to go by.

In this book, become a detective of mammal tracks and signs by searching for clues in the scene. See if you can figure out what animal left the tracks and signs, and then turn the page to see if you are right!

1

What mammal
makes a home here?

Do you see the circular holes? What do you think those are from?

What kind of mammal digs for its dinner?

What mammal sheds black and white fur?

Track Facts:

Claw marks are present.

The tracks show five distinct toes.

1.5"

1.25"

The hollow log looks like a lovely place for this mammal to sleep.

Something ate berries and took bites out of the mushrooms.

This mammal loves to eat nuts, vegetables, and fruits.

Did you guess that a skunk was here?

Characterized by their black-and-white fur, these slow-moving animals live along forest edges, woodlands, grasslands, and deserts. Skunks usually nest in burrows they build themselves or borrow abandoned burrows constructed by other animals, but they also live in hollow logs or even abandoned buildings.

Quick Facts

- The skunk family includes 10 species of skunks found in North and South America and 2 species of stink badgers found in Southeast Asia.

- The official name for the skunk family is Mephitidae, which means "stink."

- Although the most common fur color is black and white, some skunks are brown or gray, and a few are cream-colored.

- Some skunks are striped, and some are spotted or have swirl patterns on their fur.

- A group of skunks is called a surfeit.

Skunks are nocturnal, meaning they rest during the day and hunt at night. Even if you don't see the skunk in the daylight, you can tell that a skunk has been hunting for food the night before by the holes it digs while searching. Since skunks have poor vision, they hunt by hearing and smelling. Using their long front claws, they dig perfect circles in the dirt while scavenging for grubs and earthworms to eat. They also enjoy plant roots, fungi, fallen nuts, and fruit. They have even been known to enjoy leftover food from a trash can that another animal has already tipped over, as they do not climb well enough to tip one over themselves.

Have you ever smelled a skunk? Skunks are well known for their horrible-smelling spray, which is a defensive tactic used to deter other animals from making them into a meal. For this passive animal, spraying is not the skunk's first line of defense. Since it will take up to 10 days for the skunk to regenerate its spray, it will first try to intimidate the other animal by stomping the ground, raising its tail, squealing, hissing, and charging. Some skunks will even do handstands in an effort to look more intimidating. If these tactics do not work, the skunk will release its spray. Look out, as this spray can reach a predator as far as 10 feet away!

Track Facts:

Can you see a tuft of tan fur on a branch?

This animal left scratch marks on the tree.

The tracks show four distinct toes.

Overall round shape

No claw marks are present.

The plantar pad is much larger than the toe pads.

2"

2"

Look at the feathers! It looks like this mammal pounced on a bird.

This animal left tracks leading down to the stream where it went to get a drink of water.

The tracks eventually lead to this mammal's den.

A bobcat left those tracks and signs!

The bobcat got its name because of its short—or "bobbed"—tail. Bobcats are medium-sized cats, weighing between 13 and 30 pounds. Even though there are much larger wild cats than these, bobcats are very skilled and proficient hunters and are able to hunt and kill prey up to eight times larger than themselves, including deer. When smaller prey is available, though, they generally eat birds, mice, rabbits, squirrels, bats, and other small game. Bobcats, like other species of cats, sharpen their claws by scraping them on trees.

Quick Facts

- Bobcats can adapt to most habitats, especially areas with plenty of cover. They prefer rock piles and rock ledges for dens.
- They live in the United States, Northern Mexico, and Southern Canada.
- In the wild, most bobcats live around 10 to 12 years.
- Like most cat species, bobcats are very stealthy; they are able to sneak up on prey unnoticed. They can also leap a distance of 10 feet or more!
- Bobcats are playful, just like domestic house cats. They have been observed wrestling with feathers and playing with blades of grass.

VOCABULARY

- Bobcats are solitary—they usually live alone.
- Along with many cat species, bobcats are mostly nocturnal—awake at night.
- Although bobcats are excellent hunters, they are also scavengers—animals that feed on whatever is available, including plant matter, garbage, and dead animal carcasses.

The Felidae family of mammals—better known as cats—includes a huge variety of sizes, from the friendly little domestic house cat to the fierce and massive tiger. All cats have amazing athletic abilities and are beautiful to watch.

Cat tracks show four toes and a larger plantar pad in each print. The paw prints are mostly round or wider than they are long. (Dog tracks are usually longer than they are wide.) Cats have sharp and strongly curved claws for grasping and climbing, but they retract their claws while walking and running, so claw marks usually do not show in prints. Tracks from cats of different species are very similar, but the size of the paw is the biggest clue.

What mammal caused this mess?

10

Track Facts:

This mammal lives near people. It also must be a good swimmer!

Is this mammal a carnivore (eats meat), herbivore (eats plants), or omnivore (eats meat and plants)?

Claw marks are visible.

Both the front and hind tracks show five toes.

The front tracks look similar to the shape of a human hand.

Front

Front

The hind tracks look similar to a human foot with long, widely spaced toes.

The tips of all the toes are bulbous.

Hind

Did this animal get food by hunting, gathering, or scavenging?

Can you see where this animal left any fur? What color is it?

The print of the toes and plantar pad are connected, not separate.

Hind

4"

2"

A raccoon got into the garbage!

Raccoons are very common throughout the United States and Southern Canada, but they can also be found in parts of Europe and Asia. Some live in wild areas, but most live near human populations where they can live off scraps left in garbage cans, pet food left out for dogs and cats, eggs from chicken coops, and more. They are omnivores—eating plants and meat—and find nourishment from insects, eggs, small mammals, fruit, seeds, and even garbage. Raccoons are nocturnal, but they can be seen out and about during the day sometimes. They are also solitary, but a mother raccoon will keep her gaze—or nursery—of three to four babies close by her side. She teaches them how to survive and what to eat until they are old enough to survive on their own.

Quick Facts

- Raccoons average about 2.5 feet long, including their easily distinguished "ringtails," and weigh anywhere between 10 and 60 pounds! Raccoons living in colder climates are bigger and heavier than raccoons in warmer climates.

- Raccoons make a wide variety of sounds, including hisses, purrs, growls, and whistles.

- They are excellent climbers and swimmers.

- Although raccoons are adorable, they can transmit rabies, roundworms, and other diseases to humans. They also have sharp teeth and claws and are not safe to approach.

- The average raccoon living in the wild will live up to about five years, though they have been known to live four times longer in captivity.

Raccoons are great at finding homes in various environments, ranging from hollows in trees to abandoned vehicles. In the winter, raccoons go into a state of torpor—a phase of inactivity and lethargy.

Their human-like hands and fingers are excellent at grabbing things and at opening shells, doors, and trash cans.

? What mammal zigzagged from rock pile to rock pile?

The rocks shelter this mammal from the weather and predators and also provide a sturdy place to rest.

What a safe place for this mammal to hide!

Track Facts:

Claw marks are visible.

Front

0.5"

0.5"

The tracks show five distinct toes.

The tracks are so tiny! How big are they compared to your hand?

This little mammal's tail dragged in the snow! See the marks?

This mammal left scat (droppings) in its trail

It looks like a small rope piled on itself.

Look! It's a weasel!

Found across the world, except for Antarctica, Australia, and most oceanic islands, weasels live in a variety of habitats, from abandoned burrows to rock piles. They can live just about anywhere as long as the location is safe and has lots of options for food. These little mammals eat over 40 percent of their own body weight each day! You can find them in forests, grasslands, sand dunes, and sometimes even in your backyard.

These long, slim-bodied mammals have short legs and five small, clawed toes on each foot. Their necks are long, with small heads and eyes. This weasel has brown fur with paler fur on its belly, though some weasels will shed their brown fur and grow white fur in the winter to blend in with the snow. These weasels will often retain a bit of black, either on their faces or the tip of their tails.

When a weasel has white fur, it is called the "ermine" phase. Do you see how this works to camouflage the weasel in the snow?

- There are 17 species of weasels.
- Weasels have a lifespan of 2 to 3 years in the wild or up to 10 years in captivity.
- Depending on the climate and season, they may be nocturnal—active at night—or diurnal—active during the day.
- They are known to be territorial by defending their home ranges when invaded.
- A group of weasels can be called a boogle, gang, pack, or confusion.
- Much like their skunk relatives, weasels can release stinky liquid from their anal glands as a defense mechanism or to mark their territory.

Have you ever seen a weasel dance? Weasels will sometimes perform a "weasel war dance" when they have their prey cornered. While scientists aren't sure why some weasels do this, they believe the hopping, twisting dance is meant to distract and confuse the prey.

Weasels are carnivores, and they are terrific hunters. With their keen senses of sight, smell, and hearing, they hunt their prey by climbing, swimming, and running. They hunt small mammals like squirrels, mice, and rabbits, as well as frogs, birds, lizards, and insects. Weasels will often kill more than they can eat at once and then store the meat to snack on it at a later time. The least weasel, weighing between one and eight ounces, is the smallest mammalian carnivore in the world.

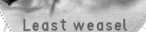

Least weasel

What mammal lives here?

18

This mammal is still active in the winter (not hibernating).

What do they look like?

This mammal left droppings in its tracks.

Track Facts:

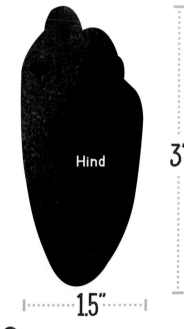

The hind feet are much larger than the front feet.

Hind

Hind

3"

1.5"

Though the toes in the individual prints aren't very defined, the track pattern is very distinct, with the larger hind feet landing in front of the smaller front feet.

Front

Front

Do you see this mammal's burrow?

A cottontail rabbit left those tracks!

Cottontail rabbits are part of the Leporidae family, along with jackrabbits and snowshoe hares. Rabbits and hares hear very well with their characteristic large ears. The bottoms of their feet are covered with strong, springy hairs that cushion their landing as they hop. Those hairs also make rabbit and hare footprints less distinct than other animal footprints. Rabbits and hares do leave very distinct track patterns, though. As they run, their large, powerful hind feet land in front of their front feet and launch them into their next stride.

VOCABULARY

- Prey: hunted
- Predators: hunters

You can see in this photograph of a jackrabbit how the larger hind feet land in front of the smaller front feet.

Rabbit droppings are small, firm, round pellets. They are excellent soil fertilizer. Many people around the world put rabbit droppings on their gardens to help the plants grow. Whenever you wonder what animal was here, droppings are a great clue!

Look at the differences between the prints of the cottontail, jackrabbit, and snowshoe hare.

Which one do you think runs across the top of snow the best?
Which one looks like it has the most power to leap far?

- A female rabbit is called a doe, a male is called a buck, and the babies are called kits (or kittens).

- Baby rabbits are born with their eyes closed and without fur, but baby jackrabbits and hares are born with their eyes open and with fur.

- Rabbits and hares are herbivores (plant eaters).

- As prey animals, those that are hunted by predators, snowshoe hares stay camouflaged by changing color—from brown in the summer to white in the winter!

Cottontail Hind Foot

Jackrabbit Hind Foot

Snowshoe Hare Hind Foot

HARE

COTTONTAIL

21

Who has been snacking on the apples in the orchard?

22

Track Facts:

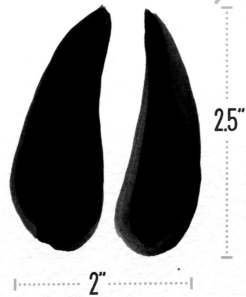

Who took bites out of the apples?

It must have jumped over the fence! Do you see the hairs?

This is the print of a cloven hoof.

Cloven means divided in two.

2.5"

2"

Something has been rubbing the bark off some of the trees.

Don't forget that droppings are always a great clue.

Oh dear ... it was a deer!

Deer are very social mammals that live in groups called herds. These beautiful mammals are herbivores, meaning they only eat plants. They can be found all over the world—except for Australia and Antarctica. Deer make their homes in wetlands, forests, grasslands, rainforests, scrublands, mountains, and even urban settings if their natural habitat is taken over by humans. Herds of deer tend to stick close to their main home and travel only around four square miles when foraging for food, finding safe places to sleep, and seeking a mate.

Have you ever seen a deer stop when it senses something around it? Deer are able to examine their surroundings without moving their bodies. Since their eyes are on the sides of their heads, deer have up to a 310 degree view of their surroundings with the only blind spot being directly behind them. Deer are also able to rotate their ears to hear sounds around them, which allows them to gather a great amount of sound as well as pinpoint where that sound is coming from.

Quick Facts

- While deer can be found in most places around the world, Africa has only one native species of deer on the entire continent, the Barbary stag.
- In the fall, many species of deer rub their antlers on trees to shed them. They will grow new ones!
- Deer are great swimmers.
- As long as a deer fawn stays out of sight, it will go undetected by predators. This is because deer fawns do not have an odor.

Do you know what a red deer, a moose, a reindeer, and an elk all have in common? They are all part of the deer family! Deer can be found in a wide range of sizes and colors, though most people think of a brown animal with tall antlers when they picture a deer in their mind. The smallest deer is the southern pudu (native to Chile and Argentina), which weighs only about 20 pounds and is 14 inches tall. The largest deer is the moose. It can grow to be 6.5 feet tall from hoof to shoulder and weigh 1,800 pounds.

Chinese Water Deer

Pudu

Elk

Moose

Reindeer

Members of the deer family are the only animals in the world that feature antlers, though antler shape, size, and texture vary widely between species. The velvety antlers of the moose are the largest antlers of all species of deer; they grow up to six feet wide and weigh up to 70 pounds! All male deer have antlers, with the exception of the Chinese water deer, which have tusks. While typically only male deer grow antlers, reindeer are an exception; female reindeer have antlers too.

25

It must be good at survival!

Do you see the bones left from its meal?

Track Facts:

Claw marks may be visible.

2.5"

2"

Front

Hind

The tracks show four distinct toes.

It is shaped like a rope and full of fur, indicating that this mammal has been eating other mammals.

Do you see the pile of scat (droppings) on the ground?

Did you guess that a coyote has been here?

A coyote is a member of the canine (dog) family. The scientific name, Canis latrans, actually means "barking dog." Native to North America, coyotes can now be found from Alaska to Panama. Coyotes have a narrow snout, and their fur is brown and yellowish gray with a white or gray undercoat. Their legs are reddish brown, and they have a fluffy, black-tipped tail.

While coyotes have a lot in common with both wolves and dogs, there are several characteristics that distinguish them from other canines. Coyotes have a more pointed muzzle and a flatter forehead than other canines and appear to have skinnier, longer legs. You can tell the difference between a domestic dog and a coyote by observing their tracks.

Quick Facts

- Coyotes live in a variety of areas, including prairies, deserts, forests, mountains, and human-populated areas such as farms, suburbs, and even cities.
- Coyotes use urine to mark their territories.
- Coyotes are mostly crepuscular (meaning they are most active at dawn and dusk), but they tend to be more nocturnal if they live close to humans.
- Coyotes will eat anything they can find. They are classified as carnivores; however, their habits are omnivorous. They hunt rabbits, rodents, birds, fish, and even deer, though they will also eat fruit and grass.
- Coyotes can run 40 mph and jump a distance of around 13 feet!
- Coyotes sometimes build their own dens and other times take over those that other animals have left behind.
- Coyotes run with their tails down, whereas dogs run with their tails up.

Often the best way to distinguish between coyote tracks and domestic dog tracks is by the line of travel, more so than the track itself.

Coyotes travel in a straight line with the tracks appearing one in front of the other, whereas a dog has a wider gait with distinctive marks to the left and right of a line. Coyotes also take longer steps than dogs, so the space between their tracks is longer.

COYOTE — Long stride — Narrow gait

DOG — Short stride — Wide gait

Coyotes are very vocal and have many ways of communicating with one another: a woof to communicate a threat nearby and get the pups back into the den; a growl to ward off any lurking danger; a huff—which is a sound the coyote makes by puffing air out of its nose and mouth at the same time—to tell another coyote to back off and stay away; a high-pitched whine when the coyote is hurt or in distress; and a bark, which can be used for many reasons, including encountering a new smell, sight, or sound that startles it. However, the most common sound that a coyote makes is a howl. Howling is used to tell the rest of the pack where the coyote is located, mainly while hunting at night. This is why coyotes have the reputation of howling at the moon.

? Can you tell which mammal made a home here?

Track Facts:

The tracks of this mammal are often blurry because the hind foot steps in the same track as the front foot, and then its large tail drags across the track.

There is webbing between the toes, which makes this animal a great swimmer.

Hind

Front

3"

5.5"

The hind foot is much larger than the front foot.

2.75"

5"

A beaver built its home in the stream!

Beavers work together to build dams made of wood and mud to stop up water in streams and rivers. These dams provide still, deep water to protect it against predators like wolves, coyotes, and bears. The water also provides a way for the beavers to float big logs and sticks to their homes for use as building material and food. Once the dams are completed and ponds formed, beavers build a lodge—their home—in the middle of the pond. Like the dams, the dome-shaped lodges are constructed with wood and mud. The entrance to the lodge is underwater, making it difficult or impossible for most other animals to enter. The den of the lodge, which is above water on dry ground, usually has room to house up to four adults and six to eight young beavers.

Beavers must constantly gnaw on wood to keep their teeth to a manageable length because their front teeth never stop growing. These long teeth are perfect for gnawing clear through trees, which are used as building material and as food.

What mammal gets to live in this beautiful park?

34

There are tiny trails between the trees.

There is a pile of pinecone cores and scales at the base of a tree.

Track Facts:

Hind

Front

Hind

1.75"

1.25"

1"

This animal uses its claws for climbing trees.

1"

Based on the size of the tracks, how big do you think this animal is?

One tree has a nest—called a drey—made of twigs, dry leaves, and grass.

Did you guess that a squirrel lives in this park?

There are over 250 species of squirrels worldwide, and they have a variety of sizes and colors. The smallest is the African pygmy squirrel, which is tiny at less than five inches long from nose to tail. The largest, the Indian giant squirrel, is a massive three feet long! This huge squirrel also has very unique coloring of black, red, and tan, with a long, bushy black tail. Imagine seeing one of those in your backyard!

250+ SPECIES of squirrels worldwide!

Pygmy squirrel

Indian giant squirrel

Of these species, squirrels are divided into three basic groups based on their body form. These groups are tree squirrels, ground squirrels, and flying squirrels.

Tree squirrel

The Eurasian red squirrel is one of 122 species of tree squirrels. This one is found in Great Britain, Ireland, and Italy, though its population has decreased dramatically in the past decade.

The golden-mantled ground squirrel looks a lot like a chipmunk. You can tell it is a squirrel because it does not have stripes on its head or face.

Ground squirrel

Flying squirrel

The flying squirrel does not actually fly; it glides by extending flaps of skin from its legs, arms, and chest. This makes parachute-like wings as it leaps into the air and glides to its destination.

All squirrels, regardless of their size, have four front teeth that continuously grow so that their teeth do not wear out despite their constant gnawing on nuts, roots, seeds, and other plants. Squirrels will also hunt and eat other small animals, such as caterpillars and insects.

? What mammal roams this forest?

Track Facts:

Compare your hand to these tracks. How big do you think this mammal is?

Sometimes claw marks from this mammal are visible in the track, and sometimes they are not.

There are five distinct toe pads with each track.

Do you see the claw marks on the tree?

4.5"

The hind foot is much longer than the front foot.

7"

Front

Hind

3.5"

It takes a powerful creature to knock a tree over!

What do you think left those tracks?

This mammal has been snacking on berries.

3.5"

39

Did you guess that a black bear lives there?

The American black bear is the most common bear species in the world. Weighing anywhere between 100 and 600 pounds, black bears are huge, but they are not the largest bear species. The grizzly bear and polar bear can grow to at least twice the size of a black bear! Can you imagine the size of those paw prints? The hind foot of a polar bear measures about 12 inches long by 9 inches wide—bigger than this whole page!

Quick Facts

- Black bears are omnivores. They eat berries, nuts, roots, insects, fish, rodents, and other small mammals.

- Black bears actually come in a variety of colors, including brown, red, blond, and black.

- Black bears prefer to live in forested areas where there are plenty of materials to make a den.

- Black bears are fast—able to run 25 miles per hour. They are also excellent climbers.

- Bears have the best sense of smell of any animal in the world—seven times better than a bloodhound dog's sense of smell (and a bloodhound's sense of smell is 300 times better than your sense of smell)!

The giant panda, a bear species that lives in the forested mountains of central China, survives on a diet of bamboo alone.

Asiatic black bears live in parts of Asia and are slightly smaller than American black bears. They are mostly herbivores, and they are incredibly good climbers.

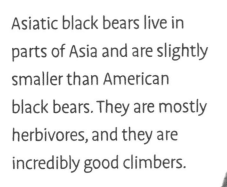

The largest species of bear, the polar bear, is considered a marine mammal because it spends most of its life on the sea ice of the Arctic Ocean. They are strictly carnivorous, with seals making up most of their diet, and they are excellent swimmers.

The grizzly bear can stand up to eight feet tall on its hind feet. Though grizzly bears do eat meat (they are excellent at fishing and scavenging for insects), the majority of their diets consist of berries, nuts, and leaves. This mixed diet classifies them as omnivores.

Now that you have become a mammal tracks detective, take notice of tracks and signs where you live. Next time you go outside, look around you. There are living creatures leaving little clues (and sometimes big clues)! Enjoy discovering how animals get food, where they find shelter, when they sleep, what they do while they are awake, and what kinds of tracks and signs they leave.

Printed in China